DEVASTATI NUCLEAR ACCIDENTS THROUGHOUT HISTORY: CAUSES AND RESULTS

Science Book for Kids 9-12
Children's Science & Nature Books

BABY PROFESSOR
EDUCATION KIDS

Speedy Publishing LLC

40 E. Main St. #1156

Newark, DE 19711

www.speedypublishing.com

Copyright 2017

The attraction of nuclear power is that splitting just a single atom can release an immense amount of power. If we can control and use that power, it's great! But what happens when something goes wrong? Read on and find out.

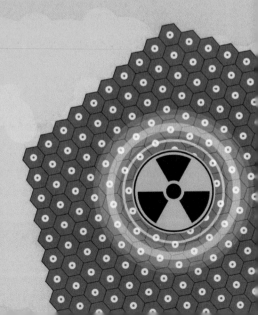

NUCLEAR POWER AND RADIATION RISK

Civilization requires power. A modern civilization requires more power than animals and human muscles can provide. The discovery in the 1940s that we could release great amounts of power in a nuclear reactor by "splitting atoms" was very exciting. The immediate result were the atomic bombs that, dropped on Japan, brought an end to World War II.

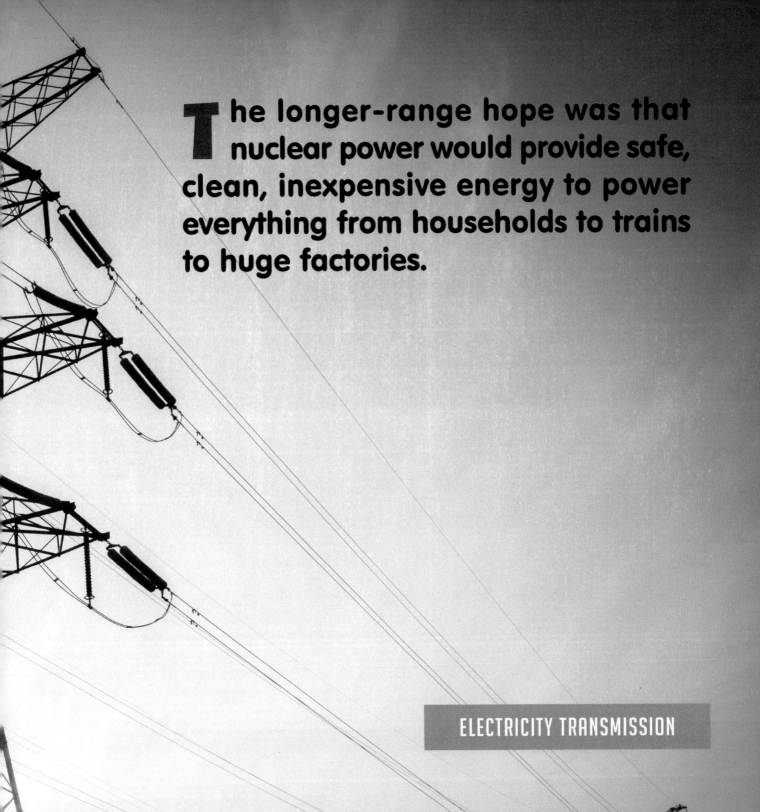

The longer-range hope was that nuclear power would provide safe, clean, inexpensive energy to power everything from households to trains to huge factories.

ELECTRICITY TRANSMISSION

There are several problems with making that dream a reality:

- Safe? There have been a series of accidents involving nuclear reactors and other radioactive material, as you will read. Some have had terrible outcomes, and some were just "close calls". But each one shows that, even with the best equipment, the best teams, and the best planning, things can go terribly wrong.

NUCLEAR EXPLOSION

AIR POLLUTION

- **Clean? The claim is made that nuclear reactors have less impact on the environment than burning coal or oil. However, the basis of the claim is flawed. It does not take into account the environmental costs of mining and transporting the uranium that fuels the reactors, the costs of building the reactor, and the "downstream" costs to the environment of having to absorb the heated water and steam that flow from the reactor, even if they don't carry radiation.**

- Inexpensive? Renewable energy sources such as solar and wind power systems are less expensive per unit of power than are nuclear power plants. And that calculation does not take into account the storage costs: "spent" nuclear fuel is still highly radioactive, and will remain that way for thousands of years. All of the cost and implications of having to safely store that material needs to be added into the cost of generating power through nuclear energy.

RENEWABLE ENERGY

TIDAL WAVES

HOW AN ACCIDENT HAPPENS

As you can see from the following examples, there can be a variety of reasons an accident happens. Not all of them can be avoided:

- Poor location: If you put a nuclear reactor above a fault line in the earth, or near a seacoast, there is little you can do to prevent damage from an earthquake or a tidal wave.

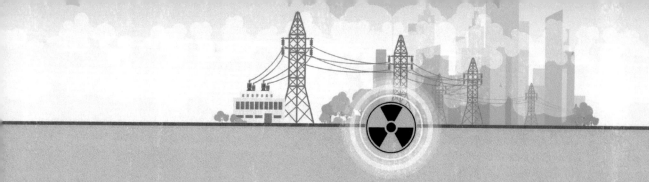

- **Poor training: Many accidents have happened because staff did not have the training they needed to do what they had to do, so they made mistakes. Those mistakes were often fatal.**

WORKER AT A POWER PLANT INSPECTING OUTPUT.

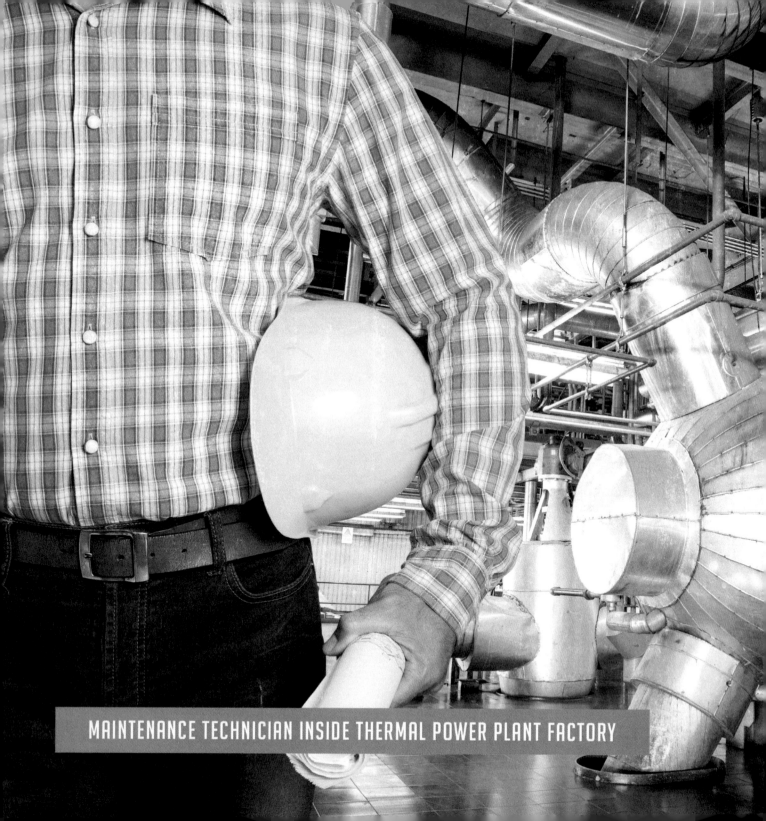

MAINTENANCE TECHNICIAN INSIDE THERMAL POWER PLANT FACTORY

- **Equipment failures: Even with the best manufacturing and the best maintenance, equipment will fail. The more complicated the system, the larger the problem when some part of it fails. And what do you do if two pieces of equipment fail at almost the same time?**

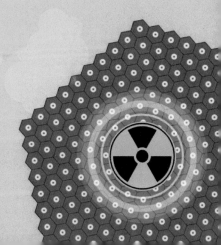

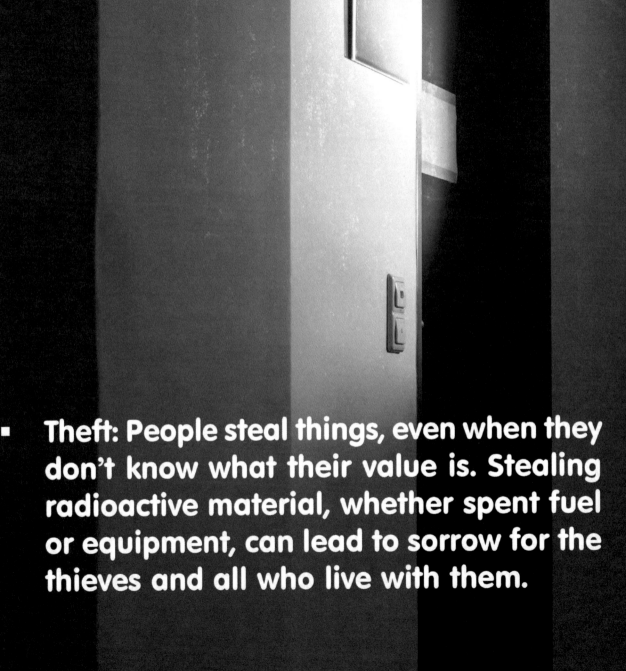

- **Theft: People steal things, even when they don't know what their value is. Stealing radioactive material, whether spent fuel or equipment, can lead to sorrow for the thieves and all who live with them.**

THIEF

MAP OF JAPAN

THE WORST ACCIDENTS

FUKUSHIMA - JAPAN, 2011

The Fukushima Dai-ichi nuclear power plant was on the east coast of Japan. In March, 2011, there was an earthquake in the area that cut off power to the plant. Then there was a tsunami, a huge wave in the ocean. The plant builders had provided a wall to protect against expected tsunamis, but this wave was two times higher than the wall.

The water crashed over and through the wall, knocking out the backup generators that had been providing electricity during the power blackout. The backup batteries soon ran out of power and the fuel in the plant's reactor started to overheat. There were explosions of hydrogen gas that damaged three of the buildings in the complex.

NUCLEAR PLANT IN JAPAN

WATER POLLUTION

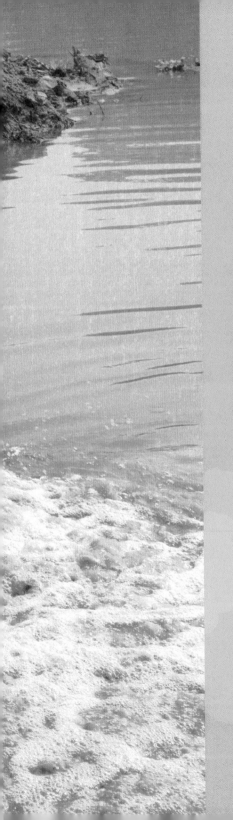

F uel rods melted in three reactor cores, and the reactors started emitting radioactive gas. Radioactivity also polluted the sea water and the land around the plant.

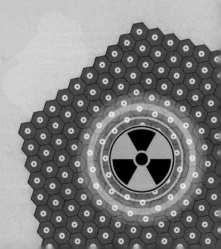

Over five hundred thousand people had to leave their homes, and the economic cost of the reactor meltdown is estimated at almost $200 billion. This is on top of the massive damage caused by the earthquake and tsunami, in which more than 15,000 people died.

TSUNAMI IN FUKUSHIMA JAPAN

GENERAL VIEW OF CHERNOBYL NUCLEAR POWER STATION

CHERNOBYL - UKRAINE, 1986

This was the worst nuclear disaster so far. It happened in a Ukraine nuclear power station in 1986. Unit Four of the reactor was supposed to be turned off for maintenance.

The team decided to run a test to make sure there would be enough electricity to run the reactor cooling system if the main power system failed and before the backup power system got running. The workers who were doing the test did not understand what might happen, and did not take all the safety measures they should have taken.

THE UNFINISHED AND ABANDONED COOLING TOWER OF THE 5TH BLOCK OF THE CHERNOBYL NUCLEAR POWER PLANT

There was a power surge that caused explosions. The explosions destroyed the reactor and caused fires in its building. Huge amounts of radiation escaped in plumes of gas and affected wide areas of the Ukraine, western Russia, and other countries. Over two hundred thousand people had to leave their homes, and a large part of the Ukraine is not safe for human habitation.

ABANDONED CARS IN PRIPYAT PARK, CHERNOBYL, UKRAINE

It took more than 500,000 workers to prevent a complete nuclear meltdown and to contain the spread of radioactive material. Many of those workers died as a direct result of contact with the reactor or the leaking material. Many other people died over the following years from cancers caused by radiation exposure.

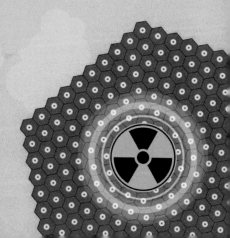

The cost of the accident was over 18 billion rubles, plus untold costs in shortened lifespans, birth defects, and other side effects of the meltdown.

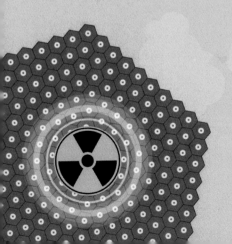

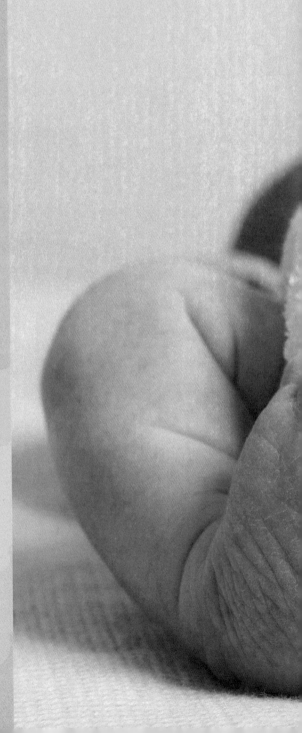

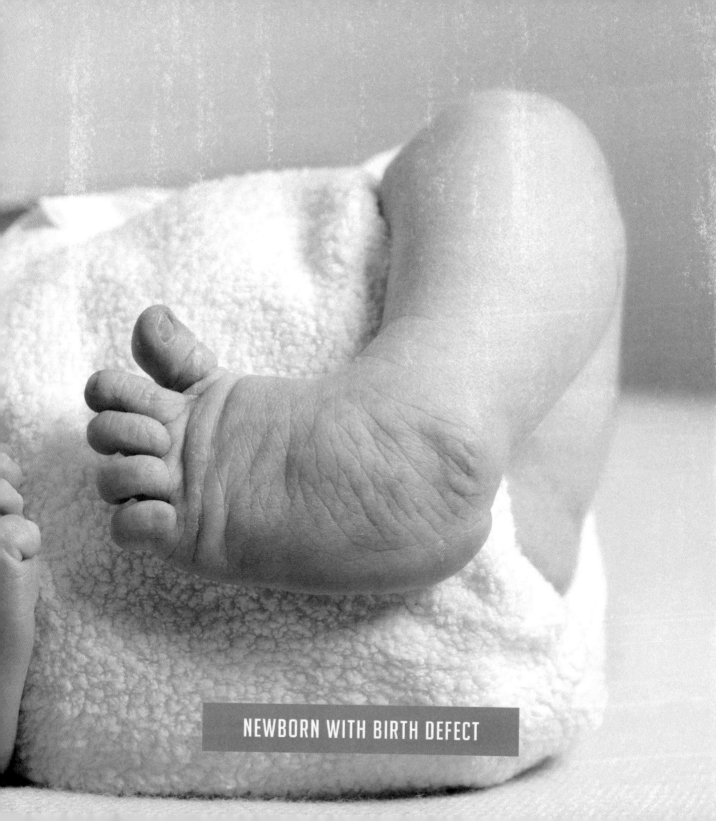

NEWBORN WITH BIRTH DEFECT

THREE MILE ISLAND - UNITED STATES, 1978

Although the partial meltdown of Unit 2 at the Three Mile Island nuclear reactor in Pennsylvania only released a small amount of radioactive material, it could have led to a serious disaster.

THREE MILE ISLAND NUCLEAR POWER GENERATING PLANT, PENNSYLVANIA

REGULATING STATION WITH PRESSURE RELIEF VALVES

There was a failure in a backup system at the reactor. The team on duty did not understand what was happening at first, and someone opened a relief valve that got stuck in the "open" position. There was a warning light that came on, but something was in between it and the operator, so the team did not know that the next steps they took would make things worse, not better.

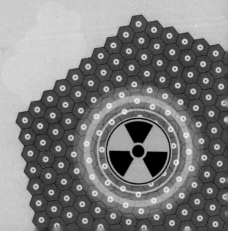

The team thought there was too much coolant in the system, when the reverse was true, and they almost drained enough coolant to cause an irreversible melt-down. Fortunately, the team was able to bring the reactor back under control, but with the loss of a lot of radioactive coolant.

NUCLEAR COOLING TOWER

FIRST NUCLEAR REACTOR AT THE UNIVERSITY OF CHICAGO

ENRICO FERMI UNIT I - UNITED STATES, 1966

The Enrico Fermi reactor in Michigan was the only operating reactor of its type, involving liquid metal. Vibrations through the structure of the reactor loosened a component. The component fell into the flow of coolant and was carried along until it blocked a nozzle. The temperature of the reactor climbed steeply, and several parts of the reactor system melted. The reactor was shut down successfully, but never again operated at full capacity.

GOIANIA - BRAZIL, 1987

A hospital in Goiania, Brazil was closed, but some of its equipment was still in the buildings. In 1987 thieves broken in and stole a radiotherapy unit which had radioactive material still in it. Many people saw, touched, or were near the unit while the thieves tried to sell it, and four people died from radiation poisoning. More than one hundred thousand people had to be tested for radioactive contamination, and almost 250 had to be treated.

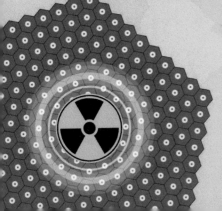

HAND WITH SKIN DISEASE. RADIATION SICKNESS.

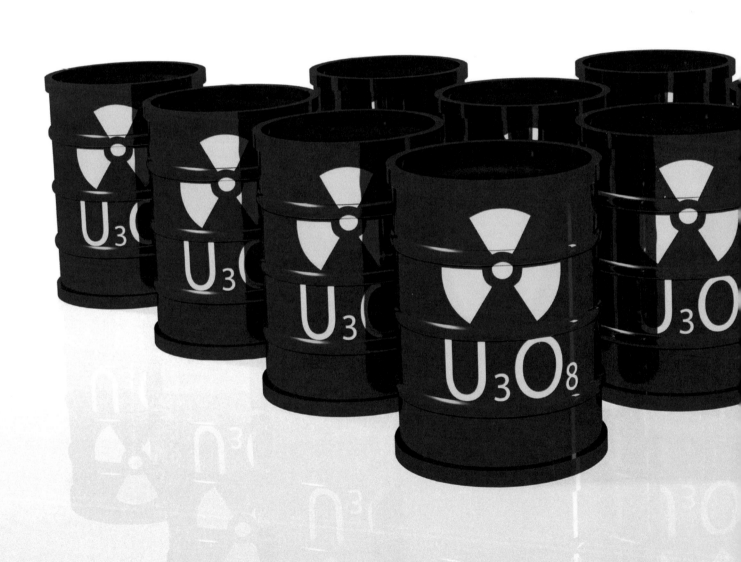

WINDSCALE - UNITED KINGDOM, 1957

A unit of the Windscale nuclear power plant in northern England went through a process to release stored-up energy. The team did not understand that the fuel was cooler than they had thought, and took steps that raised the temperature suddenly. Eleven tons of uranium in the reactor caught fire.

It took three days for workers to put out the blaze, and during that time the reactor was venting radioactive gas across northern England and western Europe. More than two hundred people died as a result of exposure to the radiation leaking from Windscale. It is considered the worst nuclear event in western Europe.

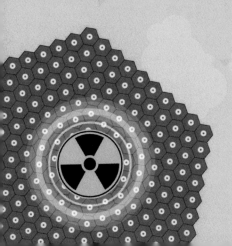

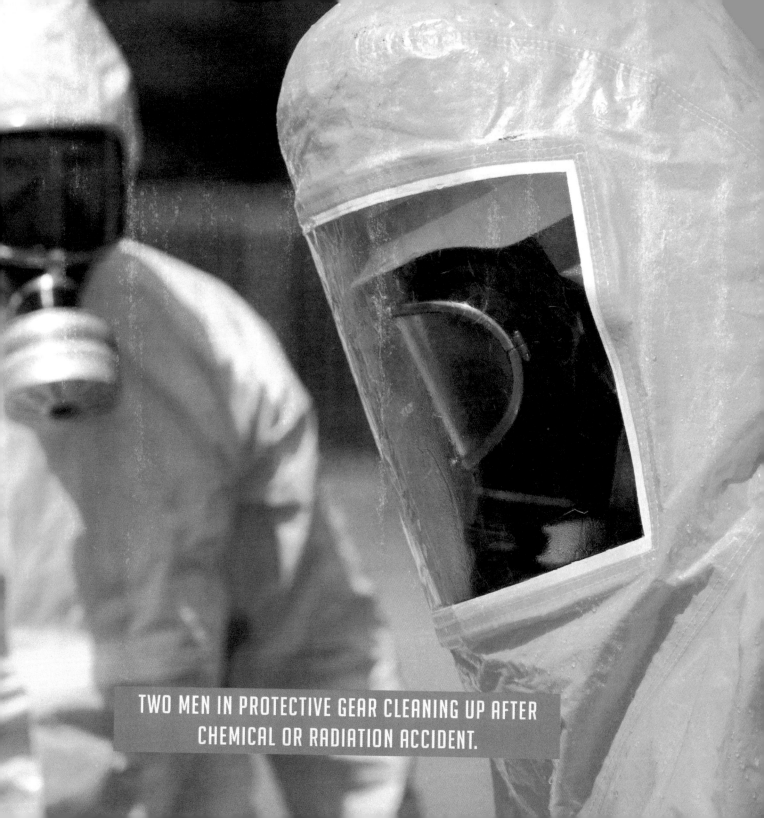

TWO MEN IN PROTECTIVE GEAR CLEANING UP AFTER
CHEMICAL OR RADIATION ACCIDENT.

THE WORKER ON A LOADER LOADS A BARREL WITH NATURAL URANIUM

TOKAIMURA - JAPAN, 1999

At the Tokaimura nuclear reactor, workers who were not trained for the task were filling a tank with highly-enriched uranium. They put more in the tank than it could contain. Almost sixty workers were exposed to high levels of radiation, and two died immediately. More than twenty people near the plant were also exposed, and an area around the plant had to be evacuated.

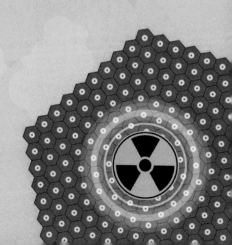

SL-1 - UNITED STATES, 1961

There was an experimental power station in Idaho. Workers were getting ready to insert test equipment into the reactor core, and they lifted the central control rod, which regulates the nuclear reaction, twenty inches instead of four inches. The reactor immediately starting generating about six thousand times as much power as it was supposed to.

IDAHO NATIONAL LABORATORY'S ADVANCED TEST
REACTOR CORE POWERED UP

Nuclear fuel turned directly into vapor, creating a radioactive steam bubble. The bubble forced the reactor out of its supports, and it bounced off an overhead crane. Coolant and radioactive fuel spilled. All three members of the team working on the reactor died from radiation poisoning.

DANGEROUS TIMES

Man-made disasters are not the only things we have to prepare for. The Earth can send us violent and scary events! Read about them in Baby Professor books like The Eruption of Mt. St. Helens, Dangerous Weather Phenomena To Look Out For!, and Ocean Tides and Tsunamis.

Visit

BABY PROFESSOR
EDUCATION KIDS

www.BabyProfessorBooks.com

to download Free Baby Professor eBooks and view
our catalog of new and exciting Children's Books

Made in the USA
Middletown, DE
06 September 2023

38123559R00038